My First ACROSTIC

London Poets

Edited by Lynsey Evans

First published in Great Britain in 2015 by:

Remus House
Coltsfoot Drive
Peterborough
PE2 9BF
Telephone: 01733 890066
Website: www.youngwriters.co.uk

Book Design by Ashley Janson

ISBN 978-1-78443-840-1
Printed and bound in the UK by BookPrintingUK
Website: www.bookprintinguk.com

FOREWORD

Welcome, Reader!

For Young Writers' latest competition, My First Acrostic, we gave Key Stage 1 children nationwide the challenge of writing an acrostic poem on the topic of their choice.

Poetry is a wonderful way to introduce young children to the idea of rhyme and rhythm and helps learning and development of communication, language and literacy skills. The acrostic form is a great introduction to poetry, giving a simple framework for pupils to structure their thoughts while at the same time allowing more confident writers the freedom to let their imaginations run wild.

Here at Young Writers our aim is to encourage creativity in children and to inspire a love of the written word, so it's great to get such an amazing response, with some absolutely fantastic poems. This made it a tough challenge to pick the winners, so well done to **Samuel Ball** who has been chosen as the best poet in this anthology.

Due to the young age of the entrants we have tried to include as many of the poems as possible. By giving these young poets the chance to see their work in print we hope to encourage their love of poetry and give them the confidence to continue with their creative efforts – I look forward to reading more of their poems in the future.

Jenni Bannister

Editorial Manager

CONTENTS

Hollydale Primary School, London

Kings Avenue School, London

Oasis Academy Shirley Park, Croydon

St Mary And St Michael Catholic Primary School, London

Upton Cross Primary School, London

THE POEMS

Ahh, I See A Slug!

S limy slugs.
L ots of slugs are black.
U nhelpful sometimes.
G reedy.
S uper slimy.

Moses Obiago (5)

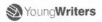

Kelsey

K ind and helpful
E njoys playing games
L oves to eat chicken and chips
S miles at Mummy
E xcited to exercise
Y esterday I did my homework.

Kelsey Brogya Mensah (5)
Chase Lane Primary School, London

Ashirah

A dorable and polite
S uper and stunning
H appy and cute
I ndigo is my favourite colour
R abia is my best friend
A mazing Ashirah
H opes that she can get her work done.

Ashirah Defroand (6)
Chase Lane Primary School, London

Nukhba

N ice and stunning at play
U nique
K ind and helpful
H ilariously funny
B eautiful birthmark on my face
A rts and crafts are my favourite

Nukhba Ahmed Saddique (6)
Chase Lane Primary School, London

Eesa Ismail

E ager to be the best
E xcited about how cool science is
S unny days make him happy
A mazing at building Lego
I s always making his sister smile
S pends his spare time reading fat books
Maths he will conquer
A rt is what he loves to do
I deas are always in his head
L oves playing football.

Eesa Ismail (6)
Chase Lane Primary School, London

Eldion

E xcited about having fun
L ove jumping on trampolines
D oing my homework
I nterested in reading books
O nly tidy up at school
N ever punch anyone.

Eldion Halili (6)
Chase Lane Primary School, London

Nyren

N eeds a pencil for writing
Y ou do your homework
R eally loves playing Kinex
E xcited about TV
N ice to play with.

Nyren Alexander Edwards (5)
Chase Lane Primary School, London

Cianna

C ianna is cute
I am interested in maths
A mazing at maths
N ever scared
N ice eyes
A great daughter.

Cianna Smith-Andrews (6)
Chase Lane Primary School, London

Max

Made in England
A mazing at times tables
X -ray vision

My mummy is wonderful
A pples are yummy and juicy
J azmin is the best sister ever
I like playing Minecraft on PS3
D iamonds are precious, just like me.

Max Callum Tahir Majid (6)
Chase Lane Primary School, London

Siya

S uper at reading and writing
I ntelligent at solving problems
Y oung girl who is very energetic
A dventurous, just like my daddy.

Siya Patel (5)
Chase Lane Primary School, London

Aleisha

A lways happy
L oves her friends and family
E xcellent at drawing
I nterested in looking at ladybirds
S uper at reading
H olidays are good because it's sunny
A mazing at cartwheels.

Aleisha Brade (6)
Chase Lane Primary School, London

Destiny

D rawing pictures
E xcited playing
S un shining on face
T errific at writing
I nterested in math
N ever gives up
Y ellow is my favourite.

Destiny Sanusi (6)
Chase Lane Primary School, London

David Orimogunje

D oes maths well
A mazing at athletics
V ery intelligent
I s not scared of spiders
D efinitely not

O kay
R emember, some spiders are poisonous
I n the summer breeze
M any children running around
O ff I go to join them
G etting along and enjoying ourselves
U ntil the rain started
N ow it is boring indoors
J ust remembered I had a new game
E xcited, enjoying and happy again.

David Folorunsho Orimogunje (6)
Chase Lane Primary School, London

Ewa Parylak

England has a part called London
Wales – part of UK too
A nd Scotland is a part of UK too

P aris is a long way away
A mazing Paris because it has a tower
R eaches to the sky
Y ears ago London burned down
L ondon is the capital city of the United Kingdom
A ustralia is a big continent
K ings and queens live in a palace.

Ewa Parylak (5)
Chase Lane Primary School, London

Carina

C lever Carina is helpful and kind
A mazing Carina is good every day
R ainbow Carina loves colours
I deas about lovely flowers
N ever gives up
A lways tries her hardest.

Carina Adu Gyamfi (6)
Chase Lane Primary School, London

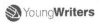

Lucy Taylor

L is for lovely
U is for useful
C is for clever
Y is for young
T is for terrific
A is for awesome
Y is for yummy
L is for laughing
O is for outgoing
R is for radiant.

Lucy Ellen Taylor (6)
Chase Lane Primary School, London

Hiccup

H iccup is my favourite character
I want to fly with dragons
C hasing dragons in Berk
C limbing high in the sky
U p, up, away up high
P eople of Berk live in peace.

Noah Nairne (6)
Chase Lane Primary School, London

Tarun

T oys are fun
A pple is red
R obots are heavy
U mbrella is brown
N est is sticks.

Tarun Sivashankar (6)
Chase Lane Primary School, London

Paige Lesurf

P is for pretty
A is for adorable
I is for interested
G is for granddaughter
E is for excited

L is for lady
E is for energetic
S is for superstar
U is for uniform
R is for rascal
F is for funny.

Paige Lesurf (6)
Chase Lane Primary School, London

Sophie Achilleos

S parkly personality
O utside in the park
P erfect sitting
H appy people smiling
I like ice cream
E legant Sophie

A mazing smiles
C lever girl
H aving fun with friends
I am eight years old
L iving with my family
L ying with Emma
E very day is special
O laf is my friend
S ophie is a superstar.

Sophie Achilleos (6)
Chase Lane Primary School, London

Dayjuan Jacob

D isco dancing
A is for amazing
Y is for young
J is for Jamaican
Uis for umbrella
A is for age
N is for nice

J is for Jacob
A is for angry
C is for crackers
O is for Oreo
B is for boy.

Dayjuan Jacob
Chase Lane Primary School, London

Teeth

T eeth are hard
E ating sweets is bad
E ating vegetables is good
T he sweets have lots of sugar
H appy teeth shine in your mouth.

Inaya Miah (6)
Chase Lane Primary School, London

Teeth

T eeth are strong
E ating healthy food is good
E ating sweets is bad
T eeth come out
H ow can you make your teeth well?

Timur Tarakci (6)
Chase Lane Primary School, London

Teeth

T eeth are for biting
E at good food
E veryone should look after their teeth
T eeth are tough
H ealthy food makes happy teeth.

Chesna Ehiorobo (6)
Chase Lane Primary School, London

Teeth

T eeth are tough
E ating and chewing
E ating sweets is very bad
T oothpaste and toothbrush
H appily taking care of teeth.

Malakie Penman (6) & Elena
Chase Lane Primary School, London

Teeth

T eeth are tough
E at healthy food
E at well
T oothpaste and toothbrush
H appy teeth.

James Readman (6)
Chase Lane Primary School, London

Little Brother

L oud and lazy is my brother!
I still love him very much
T ogether we are a team
T ogether forever, sister and brother
L ikes creepy crawlies, yes he does. Yuck!
E verything thing he does is funny and a little annoying

B ossing me around is his style
R aspberry and strawberry are his favourites
O h dear. I forget to mention he is a Batman fan
T he wrestler he likes is John Cena, *pow, pow!*
H e's a right little mummy's boy
E ating sweets all the time, even when Mum says no.
R at-a-tat – my little brother is the best.

Zahra Zaheer (7)
Chase Lane Primary School, London

Fashion

F un and fabulous
A lways looking good
S hiny, glittery, sparkly dress
H urry up and get the show on the road
I like to catwalk
O n and on I go
N ow look at me, fashionista on the road.

Eboni Trotman (7)
Chase Lane Primary School, London

Summer

S unshine is beautiful
U nder the shade we stay to keep cool
M aking sandcastles on the beach is fun
M mm, yummy strawberry milkshake
E ating delicious ice creams
R eally don't want it to end!

Eliana Anemouri (7)
Chase Lane Primary School, London

Rainbow

R ainbows are beautiful
A mazingly bright colours
I n the sunshine and blue sky
N ow look above you
B right colours starting to fade
O h, what a pretty rainbow
What a wonderful start to the day.

Keira Walton (7)
Chase Lane Primary School, London

Maddison

Maddi is my name
A thletics is my game
D ancing is a lot of fun
D on't have time, I've got to run
I f you see me, let me go
S o I can go, go, go
Off I go, can't see you
N o one is as fast as me.

Maddison Rose (7)
Chase Lane Primary School, London

Sian McClean

S ian is my name
I n the garden
A pple
N ew friend
M ummy is my beautiful friend
C ats are my pets
C ircus was fun
L ike my school friend
E njoy playtime
A t home, making cakes
N est is a bird's home.

Sian McClean (6)
Chase Lane Primary School, London

F Is For Food

C is for cake
A is for apple
L is for lemon
V is for vegetables
I is for ice cream
N is for nuggets
D is for doughnuts
A is for avocado
B is for banana
Y is for yoghurt
C is for custard
H is for ham
A is for asparagus
R is for rice
U is for umeboshi
N is for nachos.

Calvin Dabycharun (7)
Chase Lane Primary School, London

Doctor Who

D aleks are his worst enemy
O utside the blue box looks small
C ome inside and see the
T ARDIS! (Time And Relative Dimension In Space)
O pen the door and you'll see!
R ose Tyler used to travel with him

Watch and listen – the magic sound
H e travels through time and space
O ver the planets and into the stars.

Samuel Demir (7)
Chase Lane Primary School, London

Kacper Nalepka

K iwi is green
A lex is my cousin
C hildren like to play together
P aris is the capital of France
E mergency exit
R ead the books

N is for nice
A is for April
L is for lion
E is for elephant
P is for parrot
K is for key
A is for Africa.

Kacper Nalepka (7)
Chase Lane Primary School, London

Holidays In The Sun

H olidays are so much fun
O ff on an aeroplane we must fly
L ollies are yummy in my tummy
I n the sea we will splash
D on't forget to put your sun cream on
A s the sun can be very hot
Y ou can eat yummy food
T ime to build a sandcastle
I n the evening we can watch a show
M y favourite is jumping into the pool
E ngland, here we come!

Evie Lily Moffat (6)
Chase Lane Primary School, London

Birthday

B ring a present for the lucky girl
I nvite your friends to enjoy your party
R emember to have lots of fun
T aste the yummy chocolate cake
H ave a nice day at your birthday
D ecorate your party with lots of balloons
A mazing surprises coming to you
Y our friends and family have made your day so special!

Gabriella Demetriou (6)
Chase Lane Primary School, London

Blue

B for the blue sky
L for the little clouds
U is for big, blue umbrella
E is for big, blue elephant squirting water.

Saeed Mohamed (7)
Cypress Primary School, London

Giraffes

G roups of giraffes
I t can eat leaves from branches, also eats buds
R ight at the top of the tree
A t the bottom you can see legs
F unny
F urry
E xcellent
S oft and smooth.

Ida Amono Odwongo (7)
Cypress Primary School, London

The Red Elephant

E lephants are purple
L arge
E lephant
P eople look after them
H ard to catch
A re endangered
N ice
T ake a lot of things.

Jack Ronan Glynn (7)
Cypress Primary School, London

Spider

S pooky creatures
P uny but mean
I 've seen one before
D eadly and unclean
E ats its prey
R eady to bite you, I think it may.

Samuel Ball
Cypress Primary School, London

Pollen

P ollen comes from flowers
O lives grow on trees
L ife comes back
L ove is like spring
E lephants don't like it
N ow snow is there.

Ben Van Heyningen (6)
Heathbrook Primary School, London

Spring Night's Dream

S pring is as hot as a frying pan
P ollen makes you sneeze
R ain is wet
I ndigo is in the rainbow
N ice flowers
G o to the park.

Max Pattison (5)
Heathbrook Primary School, London

Springtime

S unshine is light
P lay with your puppy
R ain is pouring down
I play on the grass
N ight-time is warm
G reen grass.

Maddy May Lynch (6)
Heathbrook Primary School, London

I Like Summer

S unny day
U mbrellas so you don't get hot
Making waves
Making ice cream
E ating ice cream
R ainbows.

Kayleigh Terri Rose Leacy (6)
Heathbrook Primary School, London

Pollen

P ollen comes from flowers
O lives grow
L oganberries taste nice
L ots of bees come
E verywhere they are there
N oisy bees.

Luca Stannard (6)
Heathbrook Primary School, London

Summer Days

S unny days
U nder the shade
My skin goes brown under the sun
Mmm, ice cream
E eeeh, the water's cold
R ainbows in the sky.

Eleni Klinker De Morelos (6)
Heathbrook Primary School, London

I Like Winter

W is for windy
I is for nice, icy ground
N is for nice snow
T is for too cold
E is for even rainier than before
R is for running in the rain.

Ryan Tan (6)
Heathbrook Primary School, London

My Birthday Month

Windy days
I cy roads
N ice snowmen
T errific ice crystals
E normous warm coat
R ainy thunderstorms.

Oscar Woodward (6)
Heathbrook Primary School, London

Snow-Drops Blooming

S ky is grey
P ies for dinner
R hyming words are funny
I ce cream is yummy
N ight is rainy
G rowing grass is bright green.

Alex Pearse (6)
Heathbrook Primary School, London

Green Drop

S un is hot
P lants are growing
R ain is wet
I n the field I see lambs
N ice flowers everywhere
G rass is green.

Leia Reynaga-Basu (6)
Heathbrook Primary School, London

Hot

H ouse is warm
O utside is warm
T oo much sun.

Sarim Farid Kureshi (5)
Heathbrook Primary School, London

Summer Poem

S ummer flowers start to grow
U pside down flips
M owing the grass
M y mummy's birthday
E ight legged crabs
R adishes are growing.

Dexter Garbutt-Perry (5)
Heathbrook Primary School, London

Spring

S un is in the sky
P retty people at school
R ain sometimes in spring
I love spring
N ice weather
G reat.

Chenna Reid-Danlardy (6)
Heathbrook Primary School, London

Acrostic Poem

White snow on the trees
I see on the ground
N o rain only snow now
T rees have snow
E verything is silent
R ivers are snowy.

Nathnael Israel Yitbarek (6)
Heathbrook Primary School, London

Running In The Park

S un is hot
U p went the balloon
Made a picnic
Mum made ice cream
E ggs boil
R unning in the park.

Omer Tuzcular (6)
Heathbrook Primary School, London

Sun

S pring is hot
U p in the sky
N ot cold.

Ethan Truong (6)
Heathbrook Primary School, London

Spring

S o hot
P ouring rain
R unning outside
I t is not cold
N ights are light
G etting hot.

Reshane Riley (6)
Heathbrook Primary School, London

Winter

Winter is snowy
I n winter it is fun
N ights are cold
T ime to make snowmen
E very day it is cold
R aining all day.

Sydney White (6)
Heathbrook Primary School, London

Winter

Winter is fun
I like snow
N ights are cold
T ake your jumper
E very day I jump
R obots go in the snow, they freeze.

Malachi Frith (5)
Heathbrook Primary School, London

Summer

S un is hot
U mbrellas stop you getting wet
M eeting people
M elting ice cream
E ating jam sandwiches
R ain clouds.

Luke Stanton (5)
Heathbrook Primary School, London

All About Me

I ker
K ittens
E lephant
R ain.

Iker Lalangui Borja (5)
Heathbrook Primary School, London

Summer Holidays

S un is hot
U nder the tree house
M ouse is sneaking
M oody person
E verywhere is hot
R un in the park.

Yunus Oloko (6)
Heathbrook Primary School, London

Evil World

H alloween
A normal day, but people
L ike to dress up
L ike monsters
O r
Wolves
E vil
E ven
N ights.

Lennon David Liam Murphy (6)
Heathbrook Primary School, London

Sun

S ky
U mbrellas
M y name is Shania
M ay is hot
E ating ice cream
R un in the park.

Shania Moonsamy (6)
Heathbrook Primary School, London

Autumn

A pple
U p
T rees
U mbrella
M ouse
N est.

Yashuri Brown-Lobban (5)
Heathbrook Primary School, London

January

J une is spring
A t the park it is hot
N ight is short in spring
U mbrellas are wet
A pples grow in autumn
R un as fast as you can
Y ep! Run!

Theo Logan (6)
Heathbrook Primary School, London

Sunflower

S un makes the flowers grow
U nder the trees
N ice flowers
F lowers are pretty
L ong stems
O n the petals there is honey
Winter they don't grow
E very one is different
R ound the trees are flowers

Anna Hughes (6)
Heathbrook Primary School, London

Foggy Weather

F reezing cold weather
O n the road you shall be careful
G o slowly when you're walking
G o slowly when you're driving
Y ou have to look where you're going.

Mariela Muja (6)
Heathbrook Primary School, London

Spring

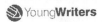

S unny flowers
P ink sky
R ed rose
I tchy
N ew baby lambs
G reen berries.

Keana
Hollydale Primary School, London

Winter

Winter is snowy and the sky is full of falling snow
I cy Icicles are so cold and pointy sharp
N ice snow to play in
T all cups of hot chocolate with marshmallows inside
E dible snowmen on Christmas cakes
R ed roses blooming, smelling nice.

Malia Diouara (6)
Hollydale Primary School, London

Summer

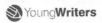

S unny and bright skies
U mbrellas not needed
M arvellous, yummy ice cream
M illions of sand grains on the hot and sunny beach
E ggs hatching out
R abbits being born.

Vega Carballo (7)
Hollydale Primary School, London

Winter

Woolly sheep going to bed
I ncredible fire warming your hands
N aughty bunnies go to sleep
T here is incredible snow
E dible snowmen
R obins wake up and dance.

Lucas Bailey-Styles
Hollydale Primary School, London

Summer

S unny skies shining everywhere
U mbrellas aren't needed
M arvellous mountain of ice cream
M illions of grains of sand
E verlasting sun
R abbits are born.

Nnauwa Emeruwa (6)
Hollydale Primary School, London

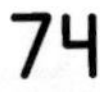

Spring

S plendid chicks hatching
P retty sky shining
R ed roses growing
I tchy grass rustling
N ew birds tweeting
G reat eggs hatching.

Kelsey Mensah (6)
Hollydale Primary School, London

Spring

S is for flowers shooting
P retty roses growing
R ed roses singing
I tchy grass swishing
N aughty lambs jumping
G reen flowers shooting.

Mia Baruwa (6)
Hollydale Primary School, London

Spring

S unny daffodils
P retty flowers shooting
R ipe roses – pink
I tchy hedgehogs
N aughty chicks running
G reen leaves falling.

Amanda Beacham (5)
Hollydale Primary School, London

Spring

S unny sky, shining
P ink flowers, shooting
R ed roses, shooting
I tchy grass, swaying
N ew eggs, hatching
G reen leaves, swaying.

Hero Cherie Pearson (6)
Hollydale Primary School, London

Spring Is Here Now!

S weet, little bluebirds tweeting whilst perched on their branches
P retty, red roses growing quickly in the dark night
R abbits are jumping so, so high
I ncredible little eggs hatching slowly
N aughty, little, white lambs playing in the wet, green grass
G reat, green leaves on the long tree.

Ema Sukyte (7)
Hollydale Primary School, London

Spring Senses

S ome lonely bunnies hopping in the wet, wavy grass
carelessly
P layful lambs playing with kind, respectable children, happily,
in the garden
R oaring animals are playing with children in the zoo
I ncredible, beautiful daffodils swaying in the breeze
N ew lambs eating quietly with making a noise or a sound
G rand, great birds singing like a queen.

Vlad Dobre (7)
Hollydale Primary School, London

Spring Time

S nuggling hedgehogs hiding under brown leaves
P rickly bushes of
R ed roses blowing in the wind
I can see bright, yellow daffodils waving in the wind
N ew, baby chicks born,
G reen wavy grass being trimmed.

Youcef Matari (6)
Hollydale Primary School, London

Winter

White snow falling fast
I ncredible robins dashing
N aughty reindeer going away
T all trees leaving the leaves
E verywhere incredible snowmen
R ed incredible fire

Avean Hylton-Linton (6)
Hollydale Primary School, London

Summer

S unny, bright and shiny skies
U mbrellas not needed
M arvellous, yummy ice cream
M arvellous delicious ice cream
E ndless sun, very hot
R ed robins being hatched.

Kimona-Lee Allen
Hollydale Primary School, London

Spring Blooming To The Area

S weet, scented roses budding in the breeze
P rickly hedgehogs are sleeping with their mothers
R ed, wonder rose blooming from the soil
I ncredible lambs eating my daffodils
N ew chicks hatch from their eggs
G entle, little birds singing in a tree

F abulous flowers growing from the deep ground
L ovely, beautiful flowers blooming quickly
O range flowers being pulled and smelt
Windy bell flowers making a wonderful tune
E njoying blackberries growing from the trees
R ed, ripe rose blooming from the bushes.

Alicia Moore (7)
Hollydale Primary School, London

Spring Is Here Now!

S weet bay rabbits, hopping happily
P retty flowers shooting from the ground
R ough hedgehogs prickling children
I ncredible smells in springtime
N aughty baby birds flying around nests
G rass tickling children's feet

F ragrant pansies in the air
L ovely lavender
O range and yellow daffodils
White, playful rabbits
E aster Bunny holding eggs
R ed roses growing from underground.

Kayann Scott (6)
Hollydale Primary School, London

Spring Is Here!

S neaky baby hedgehogs running quickly
P retty, yellow, orange daffodils budding into flowers
R andom butterflies flapping their stripy wings
I can see the trees blooming with pink blossoms
N aughty baby animals hiding in the swaying leaves
G orgeous bunnies playing hide-and-seek in the bushes.

Ananta Ramatu Good (7)
Hollydale Primary School, London

Spring

S un shining brightly on the red, fresh roses
P rickly hedgehogs snuggling in deep, dark nooks
R ed, beautiful butterflies flying in the sky
I can see wavy, swaying, green grass
N ew eggs ready to be hatched
G reen leaves growing on the tree.

Samuel Agunbiade (7)
Hollydale Primary School, London

Spring Is Here!

S unny skies, making people smile
P rickly hedgehogs quickly looking for bugs to eat
R ed roses shooting from the ground
I ncredible birds, building their nests in the strong, tall trees
N aughty bunnies eating the farmer's plants
G reen grass waving in the soft, warm wind.

Isabella Tabatabai (7)
Hollydale Primary School, London

Spring Senses

S weet bunnies are sleeping quietly in the afternoon sun
P rickly hedgehogs sneaking nuts and berries
R ed roses getting a shower in the sudden rain
I tchy grass scratching me
N ew flowers blossoming in the warmth
G racefully standing in the flower beds

F lowers getting ready for lunch
L ovely butterflies dancing
O range and yellow daffodils blossoming
Wild berries being eaten by a fox
E ight red cherries being saved for tomorrow
R ed roses cherishing

Haleema Kakar (7)
Hollydale Primary School, London

Spring Is Here!

S weet baby hedgehogs hiding in the sunny, green, large meadow
P rickly bushes hiding rabbits and rabbits having fun
R abbits jumping in the long, green grass
I nteresting insects exploring the glorious new flowers that are blooming
N aughty baby birds flying around a nest
G reen grass tickling my feet

F lowers like daffodils, blooming
L ovely flowers blooming everywhere
O range flowers growing
White, playful rabbits
E verywhere flowers blooming
R ed flowers are blooming in the garden.

Gabriella Nhyira Hagan (7)
Hollydale Primary School, London

Spring Time

S weet rabbits hugging their mummies tightly
P rickly hedgehogs sleeping in their cosy beds
R abbits jumping in a rabbit race
I tchy grass tingling my legs
N aughty rabbits pushing each other
G reat big roses bloom in the spring

F lowers are different colours
L ittle and big flowers have petals
O range, fragrant flower blossoming
Wonderful yellow and white flowers
E njoying fresh air
R ed flowers are so, so soft.

Thea Oluwole-Akinrimisi (7)
Hollydale Primary School, London

Spring Is Here!

S pectacular sunflowers shooting proudly from the soil
P retty baby lambs leaping and jumping, trying to catch butterflies
R unning rabbits swishing their pom-pom tail for food
I ncredible irises swaying in the spring wind
N aughty beavers nibbling the dark, brown, rough wood
G reen, thick grass being trimmed

F alling blossoms from the giant tree
L ovely lavenders
O range leaves, roses red
Wind gently blowing away the leaves from the trees
E njoying the fresh air
R ainy days make flowers grow!

Iris Francis (7)
Hollydale Primary School, London

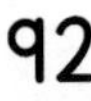

Spring Time

S pring flowers are shooting from the ground into the air
P rickly hedgehogs hiding in the spiky, green grass
R ed roses slowly blooming in the hot sun
I ncredible chicks building their nests and baby chicks
N aughty rabbits hopping around the soft, green grass
G reen grass growing in spring.

Giovanni Howard (6)
Hollydale Primary School, London

Spring Is Here

S weet, tiny, cute baby rabbits sleeping soundly with their mums
P retty, perfect, bright roses swaying in the wind
R ough eggs hatching slowly
I ncredible flowers shooting towards the sky, quickly
N aughty little bunnies hopping up and down
G igantic trees swaying left and right

F unny, little, cute rabbits jumping up and down
L ovely, prickly flowers gracefully swaying in the wind
O range and yellow daffodils
When the wind comes the flowers sway
E dible berries being picked, one by one
R ed roses.

Dajah Chapman (7)
Hollydale Primary School, London

Spring Time

S pring is when red roses start growing
P rickly hedgehogs hiding in bushes
R ed, ripe apples ready to pick and eat
I ncredible bunnies jumping up and down
N ew baby chicks hatching
G reat birds learning to fly

F lowers shooting up from the ground
L ittle chicks learning to walk steadily
O pening flowers growing
White blossoms blooming
E dible blackberries
R ed roses growing.

Abdul Rahim
Hollydale Primary School, London

Winter

Wild and windy.
I cy streets.
N obody wants to go outside.
T hen frosty fingers.
E very night is dark.
R eally wish it was warm.

Jada-Monique Marsh-Henry
Kings Avenue School, London

Summer Time

S unny usually.
U mbrellas not needed.
M oving children playing with others
M iles of kids having fun.
E xcited people going to the zoo.
R elaxing adults sunbathing on the beach.

Iris Tollett (7) & Nermen
Kings Avenue School, London

Summer

S un is hot and the weather is nice.
U mbrellas are not out and everybody's playing.
M oving children, sunbathing and relaxing.
M e and everybody, hot from the sun, will go home with smiles on our faces.
E xcited children waiting to go to the park.
R estless and constantly having fun.

Elliot Daniel (7)
Kings Avenue School, London

Facts About Winter

White snow.
I love snow angels.
N ever stops snowing.
T he snow covers the pavement.
E very day the snow falls.
R ainy looking hair.

Teejah Dixon-Morgan (7)
Kings Avenue School, London

Winter

White ice.
I love snowball fights.
N ight is sometimes snowy.
T onnes of fun in the snow.
E very day people are having fun.
R ain that stops late in the night.

Kanyinsola Salawu (7)
Kings Avenue School, London

Cool Awesome Beach

B eautiful and sandy.
E xtra relaxing.
A mazing and adventurous.
C ool down in the shade.
H ot like fire.

Zachary De Joni Rhoden (7)
Kings Avenue School, London

My Name

A mazing person.
M arvellous magician.
I ncredible young lady.
N aughty girl.
A mazing at math.

A bsolutely kind.
B ossy at times.
D elightful and dramatic.
I ncredible at art.

Amina Abdi (7)
Kings Avenue School, London

Beautiful Fairies

F abulous.
A mazing.
I ncredible.
R omantic.
I love fairies.
E nchanted.
S parkle.

Tia-Mae Nesbeth (7)
Kings Avenue School, London

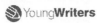

Dazzling Beach

B eautiful and sandy
E xtra relaxing and exploring
A mazing adventures
C ool down in the shade
H ot like fire.

Joyce Silva (7)
Kings Avenue School, London

Slug

S low and slimy.
L ive underground.
U gly, dirty slug.
G ross you out when you find them.

Lukas Taylor-Vincent (6)
Oasis Academy Shirley Park, Croydon

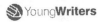

The Very Scary Spiders

S cary spider.
P oisonous spiders.
I know lots of facts about spiders.
D eadly spiders eat birds.
E at flies.
R ed spiders are poisonous.
S piders are not insects.

Niyara Hussain (6)
Oasis Academy Shirley Park, Croydon

Spider Poem

S piders are very scary.
P oison comes out of spiders' fangs.
I ncredible, some spiders eat birds.
D eadly spiders are famous to me.
E ight legs.
R ound and round the spiders go as they spin their shiny webs.
S piders are not an insect.

Lola Simkins-Manu (6)
Oasis Academy Shirley Park, Croydon

Minibeast

Minibeasts have lots of legs.
I nsects live under soil.
N asty insects.
I know lots of insects.
B ees make honey.
E at other insects.
A nts can carry strong stuff.
S tuff can be strong.
T urn your paper.

Yash Bhura (6)
Oasis Academy Shirley Park, Croydon

Minibeasts

M illipedes have lots of legs.
I nsects have six legs.
N asty slugs.
I nsects are little.
B ees make honey.
E at other insects.
A nts are strong.
S tick insects look like sticks.
T iny ants.
S tick insects can stick.

Eduardo Benavides (6)
Oasis Academy Shirley Park, Croydon

Ladybird

L adybirds fly in the sky.
A mazing and tiny.
D ancing around.
Y ellow bugs.
B usy working.
I nsects crawling around.
R acing in the green grass.
D igging in the ground.

Monique Schembri-Simon
Oasis Academy Shirley Park, Croydon

Butterfly

B utterfly.
U se feet to taste.
T ouch lots of flowers.
T ouch you sometimes.
E at lots of nectar.
R ide on wings.
F ly in the sky.
L ovely beautiful minibeast.
Y oung and old, all colours.

Nashiya Bradshaw
Oasis Academy Shirley Park, Croydon

Butterfly

B utterfly flying up in the air.
U p in the sky there's a butterfly.
T op of the roof there's a butterfly.
T ough butterfly you're brave to go up on the cloud.
E at, eat butterfly to be healthy.
R ace to the finish line butterfly.
F ly up in the sky.
L ots of butterflies like me.
Y ou are pretty, butterfly.

Eva Kormeva (6)
Oasis Academy Shirley Park, Croydon

Butterfly

B eautiful butterfly flying in the sky.
U p in the sky there's a butterfly.
T umbly butterfly so beautiful.
T ough and strong little, tiny butterfly.
E at, eat so much little butterfly.
R ough little butterfly flying in the sky.
F luffy, little, soft, colourful butterfly.
L ucky little, beautiful butterfly.
Y es you know my butterfly is so sparkly.

Safia Winnie Kuleshnyk (6)
Oasis Academy Shirley Park, Croydon

Butterfly

B utterfly fly to the flowers.
U nder the leaf they hide.
T wo angel wings.
T all angel wings.
E at leaves and nectar.
R ed wings and blue.
F ragile wings are beautiful.
L ick nectar.
Y ou are going to see one.

Tanesha Lloyd (5)
Oasis Academy Shirley Park, Croydon

Snails

S limy snails on the trees.
N o leaf juicier.
A snail has a slimy body.
I n fact all snails have shells.
L ots of slimy snails.
S nails have shells on their body.

George Cook (6)
Oasis Academy Shirley Park, Croydon

Butterfly

B eautiful and graceful.
U p in the sky.
T ired little butterflies.
T ry to fly so much.
E at lots of nectar with their lick.
R ound and round the trees.
F ly around the world.
L eaving the world.
Y ummy nectar in my tummy.

Azaliah Elliott (6)
Oasis Academy Shirley Park, Croydon

Butterfly

B eautiful, lovely patterns.
U p in the sky.
T ired little butterfly.
T ired when their wings are wet.
E at a lot of nectar.
R ound and round in the sky.
F ly around the world.
L eaving the world.
Y ummy nectar in their tummy.

Ameeza Ameerudeen (6)
Oasis Academy Shirley Park, Croydon

Millipede

Millipedes are lovely and good.
I think millipedes can tickle you.
Lovely millipedes don't hurt you.
Lots of legs.
I love millipedes.
Purple millipedes are cute too.
Every millipede is a little slow.
Dirty millipedes leave themselves alone.
Every millipede has lots of legs.

Kristian Swaby (6)
Oasis Academy Shirley Park, Croydon

Dragonflies

D ragonflies fly high.
R ed, they are not.
A pples, they do not eat.
G reen they are.
O rdinary dragonflies fly free.
N o distance too far.
F lying across the water.
L ovely, graceful dragonflies.
Y ou might see one in the sky.

Josiah Israel Andrew Powell (6)
Oasis Academy Shirley Park, Croydon

Spider

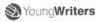

S piders don't work together.
P oisonous spiders.
I do not like spiders.
D eadly spiders are big.
E very spider has sharp teeth.
R eally spooky spiders.
S illy spiders are little.

Moeez Esaal (6)
Oasis Academy Shirley Park, Croydon

Spider

S piders have got sharp fangs.
P oisonous spiders are dangerous.
I like the spider.
D eadly spiders.
E very spider has eight legs.
R ed spiders are poisonous.

Dawid Kowalski (5)
Oasis Academy Shirley Park, Croydon

Snail

S nails are slimy.
N ice snails are normal.
A snail's shell is hard.
I love snails.
L eaves are a snail's favourite.

Alexander Gass (6)
Oasis Academy Shirley Park, Croydon

Minibeast

Minibeasts are fine.
I nsects are amazing.
N ice butterflies.
I nsects, some times they can be mean.
B ees are black and yellow.
E arwigs are annoying.
A nts can bite you.
S illy worms are slimy.
T ame an insect, if you can.

Lucas Nathanael Twilley (6)
Oasis Academy Shirley Park, Croydon

Spiders

S piders sting.
P oisonous spiders sting.
I like all small, baby spiders.
D o not touch spiders.
E very spider has eight legs.
R eally spiders suck you.
S piders build strong webs.

Kamil Kolodziejczyk (6)
Oasis Academy Shirley Park, Croydon

Daddy Long Legs

D addy long legs are big.
A daddy long legs can fly fast.
D addy long legs' wings are black and yellow.
D addy long legs live in rain.
Y ellow wings.

L egs are hairy.
O n the dark night they fly in people's houses.
N obody knows that they're coming.
G iving people webs in their house.

L ow minibeast living on the ground.
E xtraordinary legs.
G oes as fast as a minibeast.

Nasira Ricketts (6)
Oasis Academy Shirley Park, Croydon

Butterfly

B eautiful butterfly.
U se the tasty nectar.
T ouch flowers.
T winkly patterns.
E very butterfly goes places.
R ainbow colours.
F ree butterflies.
L ovely, beautiful butterfly.
Y ummy pollen.

Keeya Graham
Oasis Academy Shirley Park, Croydon

Spider

S piders crawling around.
P oisonous spiders catching flies.
I tchy spider making webs.
D izzy spiders sleep.
E very spider eats.
R ed spiders.

Elliot Jensen (6)
Oasis Academy Shirley Park, Croydon

Butterfly

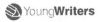

B eautiful and colourful.
U se the tasty nectar.
T ouch flowers.
T winkly patterns.
E at yummy nectar.
R ainbow coloured wings.
F ind delicious nectar.
L ift amazing, sweet nectar.
Y ummy honey.

Kezia Sauzier
Oasis Academy Shirley Park, Croydon

Spider Poem

S piders are scary, really scary.
P oison comes out of spiders.
I nsects like spiders have eight legs.
D esign their web.
E verybody knows that spiders have eight legs.
R ound and round it builds its web.

Daniele Tuffour (6)
Oasis Academy Shirley Park, Croydon

All About Minibeasts

Millipedes have lots of legs.
I nsects have six legs.
N ot all minibeasts have legs.
I n the grass.
B ees make honey.
E ats other minibeasts.
A nts are strong.
S limy slugs.
T iny ants.

George Lane (5)
Oasis Academy Shirley Park, Croydon

Slug

S limy.
L ong body.
U gly.
G ooey.

Alisa Auchaybur (5)
Oasis Academy Shirley Park, Croydon

Universe

U ranus is a planet in space.
N ear a planet, a rocket is coming into land.
I n space, there are nine planets.
V acuum is something in space.
E arth is where houses are found.
R ockets are flying in space.
S hooting stars are gleaming on my eyes.
E very planet looks different.

Szymon Kendall
St Mary And St Michael Catholic Primary School, London

Universe

U ranus has a silver ring around it.
N eptune has a baby blue colour.
I nvisible air in the big, twirling galaxies.
V acuum is a big empty space.
E arth is the Goldilocks' planet.
R ockets fly really high.
S tars are small to see.
E xciting things happen in space.

Mabel Mae Blake (6)
St Mary And St Michael Catholic Primary School, London

Planet

P eople think Pluto is a planet.
L ook in space and count the stars.
A steroids crashed to Earth in 1908.
N o one visited the hot sun.
E pic galaxies are around space.
T ake the mission to go to space.

Samee Abraar Ahmad (6)
St Mary And St Michael Catholic Primary School, London

Universe

U ranus floating with the shiny stars and all the other planets floating by.
N eptune is a blue planet that has both blues, not like the other planets.
I nvaders attacking the places on all planets even Earth and the Moon.
V ehicles are not in space because they will go everywhere, there is no gravity.
E arth is blue, green, white and brown.
R ockets zooming to space from the ground.
S pace shuttles in the station getting ready to go to space.
E ngineers go to space to explore it and have fun with the stars.

Laine Forrester Smith (6)
St Mary And St Michael Catholic Primary School, London

Universe

U ranus is a round planet.
N eptune is a cold place and it is windy.
I n Jupiter it is colourful.
V enus is a hot place.
E arth is a small place.
R ockets fly to the moon.
S aturn is a round ring.
E arth is a good place.

Sean Emmanuel Flores (6)
St Mary And St Michael Catholic Primary School, London

Universe

U sually planets spin around like a ball rolling forward.
N eptune is ice and cold just a little colder than soft snow.
I n our lively world we have lots of people.
V enus is red and hot like the sun so it is made of fire.
E arth is where billions of people live just like the country England.
R ockets flying with hot, burning meteorites.
S pace shuttles are different from rockets because rockets are smaller.
E ngland is where I live but I used to live in Brazil.

Thomas Ferrari (6)
St Mary And St Michael Catholic Primary School, London

Aayushi Jha

A ayushi is my name.
A rt is what I do.
Y ell is what I don't.
U is I love Rainbow Umbrella.
S cience is my favourite.
H ate I don't behold.
I ndia is my country; I love the most.

J umble is my passion.
H appiness what I am.
A is the letter from where I starts and ends!

Aayushi Jha (7)
Upton Cross Primary School, London

Tanisha

T anisha is my name.
A pple is my favourite fruit.
N ice and fluffy cat.
I like ice cream.
S nails are very slow.
H istory is my favourite.
A eroplanes are big.

Tanisha Rawat
Upton Cross Primary School, London

Miss Jones

M iss Jones is the best teacher in school.
I n school she is very kind.
S ometimes she goes to meetings.
S ometimes she can even get a bit angry.

J ust Miss Jones bought us a butterfly.
O n some days she can make us laugh.
N o one makes her get angry, but some do.
E veryone says that she is very beautiful.
S ome people say that she has beautiful hair.

Nabiha Fatima Mohammed (7)
Upton Cross Primary School, London

Miss Jones

M iss Jones is the best.
I n school, she helps us write.
S chool is the best because of happy Miss Jones.
S he is so smart and bright.

J oggers happily see Miss Jones when she goes to the park.
O n Wednesday she taught us spelling.
N ever yell at sweet Miss Jones.
E veryone on Earth knows she is clever.
S he is as brilliant as a science teacher.

Sophia Omidi (7)
Upton Cross Primary School, London

Spring

S ometimes it's hot but most of the time it's not.
P erhaps it rains quite a lot.
R ain, rain come again so the plants can grow again.
I n spring I go to the lovely park very smartly.
N ext spring I'm having a party because hopefully it will warm.
G reat spring, bye, bye here comes brilliant summer with
sunglasses as big as the moon!

Zara Hussan (7)
Upton Cross Primary School, London

Winter

Winter is the coldest season,
I n winter the snow is as cold as the wind because snow is made out of ice,
N obody knows where I come from,
T he winter clouds are extremely dark,
E very day you can't go to the park,
R ight everybody wrap up warm because winter is here.

Chiderah Deimante Anyaogu (7)
Upton Cross Primary School, London

Tiger

T iger, tiger, do you fart?
I t's because I know you're smart.
G rooming tiger moving sneakily when he catches his beautiful, bouncy prey,
E verybody says I am as scary as a dinosaur.
R un away because I will get you and eat you but if I like you I will play with you.

Esther Andre (7)
Upton Cross Primary School, London

Noorie

N obody is as cute as Noorie.
O nly I know her secret in the school.
O ctonauts have no idea who she is so they don't know her.
R angers who have powers is what she likes to watch and I like to watch it with her.
I magination is what she does happily with me and one of the objects she called Sir.
E xcept when we go to school we don't play with them.

Salma Allam (7)
Upton Cross Primary School, London

Malika Jones

M alika is the best, best girl, ever.
A ll the people say they want to play with me at school.
L oads of people say, 'Can I be your friend?'
I t is fantastic that people say those words to me.
K ate is my best friend in the whole world.
A ll I care about is my mum and dad, they drop me to school.

J oe is my friend, she is my best friend.
O n my feet I wear lovely shoes.
N o one says I'm horrible because I'm always nice to people.
E asy things are not hard for me.
S ome of my friends say it is easy peasy to ride a bike.

Malika Jones (7)
Upton Cross Primary School, London

Summer

S ummer is the same as the yellow sun.
U nder the sun are the shining stars.
M onday is the day when the sun has a rest.
M orning sun is going to bed then moon comes out.
E vening moon is as big as the Earth.
R eady to wake up sun, 'Yes.'

Osayuki Adagbasa (7)
Upton Cross Primary School, London

Delia

D elia is the best friend ever.
E veryone says she is nice and kind.
L ovely Delia is sometimes skipping through the classroom.
I n the playground she always plays with me.
A t school she constantly laughs.

Angelina Hussain (7)
Upton Cross Primary School, London

Football

F ootball is fun with friends.
O n Sunday I played football for three hours.
O n my birthday I had a huge football cake.
T omorrow there is a big match.
B ut I can not play football because I hurt my leg.
A nd on Monday there is a huge game.
L egs are helpful for football because what if you had no legs.
L ater my team won!

Karim Gotbi (7)
Upton Cross Primary School, London

Bikes

B ikes are the best things to play with in the park.
I n the park I always play with my bike.
K ites are cool when I tie the kite string to my bike and ride it.
E asy bikes that have stabilisers so you can ride easily.

Abubakr Raja (7)
Upton Cross Primary School, London

Cheetah

C heetahs are super fast.
H e has a spotty coat.
E xtreme cheetahs eat meat.
E xcitedly people say cheetahs are fast.
T igers sometimes fight with cheetahs.
A lmost always cheetahs eat the meat.
H appy cheetah why don't you eat rapidly?

Shahzain Butt (7)
Upton Cross Primary School, London

School

S ome people say big school is extremely hard,
C razy kids find Miss Jones very scary as a vampire,
H ow about young and older teachers should miss school,
O n Tuesday we have PE for one hour.
O ne day a cute child said, 'Can I have a shower?'
L ittle reception kids find it hard to write, so give them time to slowly think.

Kenyah Sandy (7)
Upton Cross Primary School, London

Pilot

P ilots will fly their planes.
I nside his aeroplane there are lots of passengers.
L et his aeroplane fly.
O lives are the pilot's favourite food and more.
T he pilot can fly safely.

Renaldas Zelvys
Upton Cross Primary School, London

Osayuki

O sayuki is my best friend,
S ummer is when I play with him,
A is the letter in his name.
Y ou could call him Yuki instead.
A nd you could call him Osayuki.
K it Kat is his favourite chocolate.
I love games, woohoo.

Isa Ahmed (7)
Upton Cross Primary School, London

Young Writers Information

We hope you have enjoyed reading this book – and that you will continue to in the coming years.

If you're a young writer who enjoys reading and creative writing, or the parent of an enthusiastic poet or story writer, do visit our website **www.youngwriters.co.uk**. Here you will find free competitions, workshops and games, as well as recommended reads, a poetry glossary and our blog.

If you would like to order further copies of this book, or any of our other titles, then please give us a call or visit **www.youngwriters.co.uk.**

Young Writers,
Remus House,
Coltsfoot Drive,
Peterborough
PE2 9BF.
(01733) 890066 / 898110
info@youngwriters.co.uk